What's Going on When It's

What's Going on When It's WET

by Noah Leatherland

Minneapolis, Minnesota

Credits
Images are courtesy of Shutterstock.com. With thanks to Getty Images, Thinkstock Photo, and iStockphoto. Cover – MeSamong, Studio_G, yusufdemirci. Texture throughout – MeSamong. 4–5 – Iakov Kalinin, joerngebhardt68. 6–7 – Martin Ferriz, Pokoman. 8–9 – JoshStocker899, ND700. 10–11 – Tonio_75, DELstudio, Milju varghese, Nadzin. 12–13 – ssuaphotos, Tero Vesalainen, Maike Hildebrandt. 14–15 – Sanja Karin Music, Tom Fern, FANDESIGN. 16–17 – Aluca69, bogdan ionescu. 18–19 – Sisika, Tomsickova Tatyana. 20–21 – CHOKCHAI POOMICHAIYA, Gorloff-KV, Blueastro. 22–23 – nataka, A3pfamily, TORWAISTUDIO, RicardoImagen, torwai.

Bearport Publishing Company Product Development Team
Publisher: Jen Jenson; Director of Product Development: Spencer Brinker; Managing Editor: Allison Juda; Editor: Cole Nelson; Associate Editor: Naomi Reich; Associate Editor: Tiana Tran; Art Director: Colin O'Dea; Designer: Kim Jones; Designer: Kayla Eggert; Product Development Specialist: Owen Hamlin

Library of Congress Cataloging-in-Publication Data is available at www.loc.gov or upon request from the publisher.

ISBN: 979-8-89232-873-9 (hardcover)
ISBN: 979-8-89232-959-0 (paperback)
ISBN: 979-8-89232-903-3 (ebook)

For more information, write to Bearport Publishing, 5357 Penn Avenue South, Minneapolis, MN 55419.

CONTENTS

WHAT IS WEATHER?

Weather is what it is like outside. The weather is always changing.

Rain storms can make weather cold and wet. They can also bring floods and rainbows.

WHAT'S GOING ON WHEN WEATHER GETS WET?

RAIN

The air is full of water **vapor.** Water vapor turns into **droplets** when it cools. These droplets gather to form clouds.

Water droplets fall when they get too heavy to stay in the cloud. This makes rain.

WHEN IT RAINS

Sometimes, rain can fall very lightly. It can even rain when the sun is out. This is called a **sun-shower.**

Rain can also fall very heavily. It can last for a few seconds or many hours.

HELPFUL RAIN

Rain is very important to the **environment.** Plants need water to grow. Farmers grow plants for food.

Rain also keeps rivers full. People use water from rivers for drinking and washing.

MONSOONS

Some parts of the world get **monsoons.** Monsoons are strong winds that often bring a lot of rain.

Monsoon rains can last for months. Places that have monsoons are often dry the rest of the year.

FLOODS

Too much rain makes the water in rivers rise. Rivers can even **overflow** and flood.

Floods happen when water spills onto land. Floods can cause lots of damage. Whole roads and cities can be flooded during a storm.

RAINBOWS

Rainbows often show up after a rainstorm. Rainbows happen when sunlight hits water droplets in the air.

Light is made of many colors. Light splits apart when it hits water droplets. This creates the colors of the rainbow.

FOG

Wet weather can also create fog. Fog is a cloud that is very low to the ground.

It is made when water vapor collects around dust in the air. Fog usually forms during nights that are cool and wet.

STAYING SAFE

Be careful during wet weather! Rain can make the ground slippery. Fog and rain may make it hard to see.

Look carefully before crossing the road in wet weather. Stay indoors to keep dry and warm.

RAINY DAYS

Wet weather can also be fun. Rainy days are great for playing games indoors.

You can even play outside if an adult says it is safe. Make sure to wear **waterproof** clothes!

GLOSSARY

droplets tiny drops of liquid, such as water

environment the natural world

monsoons strong winds that often bring heavy rain

overflow to spill over with water

sun-shower a light rain while the sun shines

vapor something in the form of a gas, such as water vapor

waterproof able to prevent water from passing through

INDEX